Blooming Cactus

Poetry

mikateko e. mbambo

cover art by Mikateko E. Mbambo

Mwanaka Media and Publishing Pvt Ltd,
Chitungwiza Zimbabwe
*
Creativity, Wisdom and Beauty

Publisher: Mmap
Mwanaka Media and Publishing Pvt Ltd
24 Svosve Road, Zengeza 1
Chitungwiza Zimbabwe
mwanaka@yahoo.com
www.africanbookscollective.com/publishers/mwanaka-media-and-publishing
https://facebook.com/MwanakaMediaAndPublishing/

Distributed in and outside N. America by African Books Collective
orders@africanbookscollective.com
www.africanbookscollective.com

ISBN: 978-1-77906-511-7
EAN: 9781779065117

DISCLAIMER
All views expressed in this publication are those of the author and
do not necessarily reflect the views of *Mmap*.

iii

acknowledgements and thanks

my deepest gratitude to the Universe.

kanimambo my Ancestors and my parents Monkatso and Emmanuel Mbambo – i am because you are!
      a special thank you to my soulmate, Mahlatse Langa for your inexplainable love.
many thanks to the publisher, Tendai Rinos Mwanaka for creating a platform to share this work.
      many thanks to my goddess-sister, Toyin Ajao for the conversations that matter.
i also thank my dear friend, Sibusiso Biyela, for co-designing the book cover with me.
      Lesego Masethe, for lifting me up when i am down, *thobela koko*.
and for always standing up for women and girls, Hellen Phushela, *ndza khensa*.
      finally, thank you to my late paternal grandparents, Ntombizodwa (Mama) and Magezi (Kokwani) Mbambo for coming this way.
      Mama, you echo in my voice. Kokwani, for seeing galaxies in me when everyone else saw a single star, i thank you.

dedicated to the black women
rooting

especially, **Ntombizodwa**
i have a loneliness
a deep yearning
i wish i knew your story
as told by you
and as i press forward
in the pride and strength of my womanhood
i not only rewrite my story and yours
i heal myself, you and our foremothers
many things are unknown to me
however, i am rest assured in our love
and this may well be
the only truth i will ever know
about our story

to live

i freed my voice
and this is my tenacious song

Table of contents

This is one anthology that has the power to break and mend you.
Mikateko has freed us all!

~Dr. Toyin Ajao (PhD)

so
i learnt the mysteries of the hive
the wisdom of the bee
now
i am blooming

darling i am blooming
         hive bee blooming

i know how
i know what
it feels like to be black
woman
working for institutions established by the white afrikaaner
men
i know how
i know what
it feels like to be black
woman
sitting around a table with white afrikaaner women and
men
i know how it feels like
to walk through passages that echo the agony my ancestors
felt
i know what it feels like
to occupy an executive office that echoes the atrocity my
ancestors endured
i know too well my power as a black
woman
and the afrikaaner at work never likes it

my truth

It is in the strength of my locked hair
That the oppressive white afrikaaner system
Fears the possibility of a united black nation
It is in the very might of my locked hair
That the black man
Fears the possibility of cohesive black sisterhood
And
This beautiful force that crowns my head
Is a reminder
Every single day
Unity is power
When one is supported by her people
She is strong
And the Tsonga people will attest
The strength of the crocodile is water

Locks

below my eyes
torn stories
stains
with chapters
detailing misfortune
those dreams of sustainable townships
denied
another battle reiterating the long walk to freedom
                                    access to education still
favours the privileged
this black woman body left behind
will continue to fight her way forward
covering the bitter disappointments with make up
facing this new day
revisiting those dreams
rewriting sentences
with chapters filled with new approaches
to wear around my mouth
like smiles of victory
new dreams

Misogyny with his hands around her neck
Then his fists against her head
Excruciating kicks to her belly, her spine
For
The Thing between her legs

Sexism in his egoistic acme
Looks down on her with insolence
Restricted in all extraordinary spheres
Because of
The Thing between her legs

Male Superiority though tanned with atrocity
In her Feminism armour
She will justly conquer him
Regardless of
The Thing between her legs
                    *The Thing between her legs

foremother for civil rights
for the male black body
entirely
no matter the cost
wholeheartedly
grandmother against apartheid
alongside the male black body
completely
no matter the repercussion
with all she was
mother continues the legacy
for the male black body
fully

                                       but unspeaking

she tells me
heartbroken/disappointed
the time is now/it's high time you put the black female
body first

black female body

We have emptied ourselves
And hung on the windows of our Souls
The curtains of Aloneness

Our breath wasted
In the many races we ran
Blood flowing from the soles of our feet, shaping their
path
We have sacrificed
Dreams we have carried from our very existence
To nurture those who give us up
Our Being misused
Till She herself embraced forlornness
Placed in fading backgrounds
We made our wombs their homes
They fed from our burning nipples
To contextualise us as the weaker sex
Our essence bottled
Shipped across the shores of wailing seas
Stored away and never to be freed
We were at the forefront in those racial wars
Wounded and swallowed by the earth
And in their history books we occupy just a subsection
We are conscious women
Mindful of our aptitudes
We are Power!
Remember us…

*We are Conscious Women

city lights around you
meaningless conversations
some wine to merry the heart
silencing all the conversations that matter
you deserve better
baby girl
sounds like the mother wind whispering
and deep down you know
his cocky attitude doesn't match your worth
why are you still here?
raising his glass
the smell of his cigarette stings
may we get what we don't deserve

                                            proud to see you

decline
speaking out
but sadly, for him to get it
you had to mention his daughter
            his daughter

When the earth waves goodbye to the sun
Darkness welcomes the moon and the stars
I cover myself with dream
As the heart beats
I see Black Person
Beautiful like the chiselled churches of King Lalibela
I smell Black Person
Scented like the unification of soil and rain
I hear Black Person
Echoing like the voice of Life
I touch Black Person
Strong and unbowed like Kimpa Vita
Yes
Dona Beatrice
And as the heart beats
I am Black Person
                    *Black Person

did i tell you about the little girls
living in almost all these homes
sweeping their abuse stories under the rugs
dining tables
beds
pretty much everywhere unseen
because theirs is a thick manuscript of disgrace
society tells
one to keep a secret forever
as if it doesn't grow like a baobab
did i tell you how they are shamed
even by female bodies
that held the same broom
their stories piled under the rugs
dining tables
beds
pretty much everywhere unseen

part 1
heal the girl child

i am telling you that they need not be ashamed
nor shamed
they need not feel worthless
and responsible
they need not carry the guilt that's meant for those male
bodies
who usually never account
who wipe their dirty acts on top of the rugs
dining tables
beds

                                 i am telling you to
lovingly be present in their healing journey
theirs is a remedial manuscript of restoration
now
throw out the rugs
dining tables
beds
throw out those male bodies
burn them if you must

part 2
heal the girl child

We are the ones
Our foremothers have been waiting for
To retell their stories
Our stories
Stories
We are the ones that speak
Of the baton passed down to us
Taytu Betul
Empress
Steadfast adviser
Familiar with politics
Its tricks
Have you forgotten Her Ethiopia?

We hold the words to reshape our history
To bring to life those fire place oral tales
Those never told truths of Your resistance against
colonialism
Nzinga Mbande
Queen of Ndongo now Angola

Part 1
The Glorified Lionesses

You dispositioned Goddesses
In the scriptures
We are the ones who will sing You praises
As we reposition You on Your rightful thrones
Your role against apartheid
Miriam Makeba
Will resound endlessly
Like Your timeless music
We are the ones who will exhume Your contributions
Charlotte Mannye Maxeke
Miriam Tlali, Ngwanyeruwa,
Aoua Keite, Funmiloya Kuti, Ellen Kuzwayo,
Winifred Madikizela,
Wangari Maathai

Part 2
The Glorified Lionesses

and you came to me in a dream
we danced
our feet hands
and the ground our drum
something repaired in me that night
though it tore my heart to see you dance farther and
farther away
your melodic voice fading
but i caught those last lyrics

                      'until the lioness tells her
story,

                         the tale of the hunt will
always glorify the lion'

          summoning the lioness

You are all that divine magic
Splendour
Magnificence
You are all that incomparable brilliance
Glory
Radiance
Yours and that of your Foremothers
As you firmly stand on their mighty shoulders
Never forget how they were oppressed and repressed
Queen,
That time is gone
Yours is the throne
Possess and reinstate
Retaliate

Crowning the Queen

mom asked her
why her face was bruised
swollen
bloody
i can't even see your eye
what happened

                                       she protected him

mom asked her again
why are you limping
what happened to your head
how did you break your arm

                                     she protected him
                                     she protected him
                                     she protected him

the last day mom asked her
                         but she couldn't protect him
her body lay frozen in the coffin
i couldn't tell her mouth from her eyes
so disfigured
i wished i had protected her
                coffin regrets

Here we are
Fighting for equality and equity
Battling to take part in leadership and business
Struggling to get access into prestigious programs
Here we are
Told how to wear our hair
How to cover our bodies
How to sit and how to talk
Here we are
Watching our backs on the corridors, streets and parking lots
Carrying pepper sprays, sharp objects and prayers in our bags
Walking in groups to the restrooms
Here we are
At war with so many things inflicted mostly by one thing
Men

Here we are

it hurts differently
when sisters perpetuate misogynist behaviour
femicide
rape culture
human trafficking
hiding behind mobile devices they post of how she
deserved it
gold digger
side chick
skeberesh
and the many labels they have created
as if to dig a pit
forgetting the old sayings
that whosoever digs a pit shall fall in it
when sisters are blinded by patriarchal tactics that divide
women
the same tactics of segregation
apartheid used to divide black people
reinforcing the status quo
placing shackles on another woman already menaced and
manacled

part 1
black women consciousness

i will paraphrase Steve Biko
first step
make the black woman come to herself
pump back life into her empty shell
infuse her with pride and dignity
remind her of her complicity in the crime of allowing
herself
to be misused
letting evil reign supreme in this misogynistic patriarchal
world

                          and Ellen Kuzwayo
call me woman
and in the ancestral realm
know this
i will fearlessly speak out against women who perpetuate
the
dismantling and killing of other women

part 2
black women consciousness

Mma and I cry today
For the baby girls and toddlers
Who can't fight for themselves
Raped and killed
In their homes
And other 'safe' spaces
What we hear and witness daily has left mildew in our eyes
The rust around our hearts
Makes it painful to breathe
Mma and I cry today
For the girl children
Whose stories of abuse
Are knitted
Around their wombs
For those brutally murdered
Dumped in a *swart sak*
Their bodies cut and burnt
Untitled

my friend was hostile to my boundaries on religion
harassing me
calling my magic *haram*
warning me to repent
using religion as logic to defend his reasoning
he said the male body was created by god
to lead the female body to truth
bullshit, i thought
the male body is glorified by religion
the male body has privilege
the male body is a bully
i am not the kind to submit

                      unrefined and proud
i question and interrogate
you know what they say
critical thinking
not blind faith
i speak out
silence reiterates stereotypes
silence betrays
i am too magnificent to come from a male rib
abusive religion

black men
when we are discussing sexism
please don't behave like white people
who bring up class struggles when we are discussing racism
don't

black women
jailed
for defending themselves against abusive men
deserve psychiatric evaluation and justice
far more than white boys
and white men whose sentencing for rape and murder
take forever
because they can't allocate them beds in psychiatric
hospitals
with short sentences
because they are mentally ill
justice for black women

racism is the main agenda
probably the only agenda
if political groups acted against gender-based violence
as they did with H&M stores
if it hurt men as much to see women and girls suffer
as it hurts them to hear that #MenAreTrash
South Africa would be a safe space for women to live
we matter too

love
is
my mouth
and the stories curled around my tongue
stems of the grape vine flourishing on my mother's
washing line
power
and its fruit
healing
love vine

nauseating from the fruits of apartheid
beaten to a pulp by sexism
my mouth refuses to just say
a luta continua
because now my heart knows
vitoria e certa
we might still be fighting the same battles
our foremothers fought
but don't despair black Queen
ours is victory
noma kanjani
victory is certain

it is not enough
to love and respect us because we are your
mothers
daughters
sisters
disrespecting those who don't share your DNA
how much longer are we supposed to express that
we are people
women are people

what a great time to be alive
witnessing women disrupt the system
this intensely
Yaa Asantewaa, Charlotte, Harriet, and Albertina
Victoria, Winnie, Zora, and Mbalia
together smiling and rooting
Lillian, Emma, Alimotou and Rosa Parks
rising

woman
when will you stop being a gatekeeper for patriarchy
will you stop glorifying trash
why do you continue to hold the knife where it is sharp
stop

white people at places of work
must know that we have arrived
we are our grandmothers multiplied and transformed
feel it
the arrival

why are you so enchanting
he asked
i walk around with the moon and the ocean in my womb
the universe is at home within me
she said
divine feminine

some songs reek of you
burning my bones
burning my chest
burning my stomach
all i can do is write me a remedy
memories

this misogynist culture
perpetuated in popular music
demeaning women
should be muted
turn it down

sister battling
                mental health
up and down
oh merry-go-round
trigger trigger
round-go-merry oh
down and up
                mental health
battling sister
heal

how many times have you cried
because of him
only to welcome him back
again and again
at the sound of his apology
or a gift wrapped with guilt
symbolising his apology
because he is too proud to say he is sorry
repetition

gender roles my ass
i got this
i got this
i got this
affirmation

we work so hard on ourselves
doing self-love
deepening self-love
deepening gratitude
pouring coconut oil
smudging
recharging crystals
balancing our chakras
sharing our stories
awakening
being present and centred
burning incense
and them brothers
still wilting

another gap

In a trance
She told me she was proud to
See women today
Digging deeper
Questioning the role of colonial influence in
Our cultures and traditions
Trying to piece together the puzzle of
Peaceful matriarchy
Creating anew a society that nourishes the girl child
Not leaving behind the boy child
Teaching them both alike
She told me not to slumber
To never give up
That beautiful things are already blooming
In my waking life
Like the blooming cactus

Blooming cactus

Mma
i called
had you been given the opportunity
what would have been my name
        my name

        your name
your name before i could even
think
there were to many voices
        your name

We'd say nothing to each other
Every time I started a conversation
He'd say he had a headache and wants to rest
But he always had the energy to pat kisses on my body
He'd stare at my silence
And even that made him uncomfortable
He was comfortable stroking my neck
He never answered questions
I made him nauseous
But he liked my mouth
One day
After what seemed like a beautiful weekend together
I packed my conversations
My stories neatly folded near my poems
And off I went

Today he checks in
When my body is no longer available for him to caress
He wants to answer those questions
Have those conversations
Stare at my silence with admiration
He probably doesn't get headaches around me anymore
I didn't bother to ask
Mine's a new chapter in the journey
He is not welcome
And it feels good
Free

you want to wait
till it aches on your side
piercing your heart
till it hits home
you want to wait
till it's your
        grandmother
your mother
        aunt
your sister
        wife
your girlfriend
        niece
your daughter
but we refuse to wait
because she is us
we are her
we will not retreat
bash it as you will
feminism is women's rights
 human rights

        she is us

i haven't forgotten
Thandiswa Mazwai
the foremothers
that bore us
oh Nina
i want to reflect the times
yes Lira
and speak about it
inspired

honey
you got to learn to dance with broken bones
so long as you still got breath
dance
it's our struggle song transitioning into a triumph song
learn

we are many things
race
gender
religion
class
before we are human
probably our greatest impediment
human first

i am nobody's neck
and nobody is my head
i am complete
whole

disrupting patriarchy
in this lifetime
for tomorrow women
makunyiwe by all means
female disruption

they say they are woke
but they aren't rising
still trapped in insecure masculinity
silent in times of repression against women
these black men we call brothers
trapped

you will learn
my love
to love around the hole in your heart
between the broken pieces
you will learn to mend
mend

a new day dawns
faces of women
no longer in despair
no longer afraid
new day

baby girl
fist in the air
victory is certain
you will rise and resist all forms of oppression
like Angola's Queen Nzinga Mbande
steadfast
self-assured
leading like the fearless Queen Mother
Yaa Asantewaa of the Ashanti kingdom
courageous
rise and resist

all the tears
she cries
are royal jelly
nourishing her soul
queen bee

foremothers knit their journeys
on the palms on my hands
their struggles and victories
stitched together
linage thread

the fruit of my womb
is not merely flesh and blood
it is creativity too
womb

stop telling me
to cover and support my areola
my nipples are not bait
i won't compromise my comfort
to make you comfortable
no bra

my beauty
is not for your satisfaction
when i wear my shells and beads
my high heels and high waist jeans
my ylang ylang and neroli
it is not for your desire
it is all for me
all for me

i am woman
resonating the genetic material of the first mother
walking through the thorny
paths of this misogynist world
my calabash held firmly
with dreams that never spill
no matter how harsh the journey
misogynists hiding in the nearby bushes
throwing rocks
insults
catcalling
threats
my calabash held firmly
with visions that never spill
no matter how deadly the journey
keep walking

We haven't seen her since

Taken a few houses away from home
To be smuggled out this border
Into another
Like a bag of drugs
But she breathes
She lives
Exchanged for money
Her body made a commodity
The system is not rigid enough to protect us
But strong enough to destroy us
                    Sister Trafficking

she ponders too
how she can die better
how can woman die better
assured that her fight was not in vain
that she not only disrupted the system of patriarchy
but uprooted it and its brothers
misogyny
femicide
and all that perpetrates it
assured that she leaves behind
a generation of women
who speak up
fearlessly
fearless

We watched them
Our leaders
Them both
Women and men

Political abuse
Mightier than the law

We watched them
Our sisters
Them all
Sexually assaulted and harassed

Political abuse
Mightier than the law

We watched them
Our leaders
Protecting each other's reputation
Getting away with delinquency

We can no longer just watch
Our sisters
Served no justice
Fight we will
Our leaders

you can't sugar-coat misogyny darling
ain't no time to romanticise femicide
  honey

hear me when i say this
if we were to commemorate all the women and girls
who died from the lash of men
every day would be a day of remembrance
do you hear me

  honey
ain't no time to romanticise femicide
you can't sugar-coat misogyny darling
lest you forget

I remember meeting a girl
In Sosh
Wearing torn clothes that charged a stench
I was afraid when she approached me
Then she told me her story
That we later shared with my friends
Then the police
A friend travelled to Pretoria with her from Zeerust
Exchanged her for money
Drugged
Raped
Prostituted
Till she fled
The policeman taking the statement laughed
Said she can walk back to Zeerust
Eight years later
A policewoman taking my statement
After a car chased me almost running me over
Asked if I was injured
I was assaulted
No
She laughed and told me I didn't have a case
Our police system continues to protect perpetrators
This too is police brutality

Police Brutality

i had all my qualifications in place
skills and experience
knowledge
passion
and a full portfolio
exhibiting excellence
but
he had other things in mind
my vagina
my breasts
my mouth
he said i was naïve to think my
qualifications
skills and experience
knowledge
passion
were enough to grant me a position
that i was naïve to think he was at all interested in my
brilliance
the hostility in his eyes
when i rejected his offer
taking away his power
teaching him a lesson
and sealing it with my middle finger in his face
middle finger

we realised that in our struggle
for equality
as black people
we
still have another battle
for equality
as black women

we carry black men on our backs
and in turn
they bruise and break our backs with their fits and knives
and guns

another battle

Do you ever ask yourself
What am I doing to perpetuate
The abuse of women and girls
What am I doing to keep the flame of patriarchy lit

I think it is sad to live in silence
When women and girls are being raped and killed

I think it is sad to dance mindlessly
Promoting and sharing
Content demeaning women and girls

I think it is sad to take part in conversations
Reinforcing gender stereotypes

Do you ever ask yourself
What can I do to end
The abuse of women and girls
What can I do to put out patriarchy
Thoughts

and i also think it is sad
to go about your journey
fist clenched
prepared to strike
because everywhere, everywhere
there's a man waiting to
brutalise your soul
strike

and we must create spaces
all around us
that make it hard for conversations that portray women
as objects
 to root
and be these spaces
safe spaces

but our brothers are acquaintances
of this vicious system
that oppresses even them
seen

i am potent
potion
an elixir
water and strong affirmations
concoction

i learnt earlier on
to love myself fiercely
love myself gently
and when their words poked
the acne
my face was forming galaxies
beautiful

my mouth no longer
tastes of your deceit
and my body no longer aches
from the memories
healed

you have learnt to brew
your elixir
alone stirring and stirring
patient and the heat just right
stirring and stirring
better than bethesda

lover
you are a goddess
you will learn to stretch your arms to the skies
 collect the stars and
align them above your crown
aligning

and when you battle
discrimination
chauvinism
all these bigotries
remember you are not alone
hopeful

his insecurities never slept
guarding her every move
setting boundaries and stripping everyone away
from her
marking a territory that isn't his
claiming
and behaving like he owns her

                                        it was too much

and the same talks about consent
the pictures and videos he took of her
no consensus whatsoever
the lying and double-dealings
the verbal abuse
and controlling
his insecurities never slept
but she woke
                    unbearable

And Mumbi
In the great sea Lwamumbi
On her majestic throne
spoke;

You can oppress Her
Repress Her
But you cannot wipe Her from the face of the earth
You can murder Her
Brutalise Her
But you cannot erase Her footprint
She is the granddaughter of those you lynched
Raped
      Oh, but ever-living
You must also know
While I and the Foremothers are rooting
She is blooming
When She is rooting
We are blooming
You cannot end Her
She Us!
          Mumbi wa Lwamumbi

buying bread at the spaza shop
a young man from nearby
drunk or high
maybe both
said it was a disgrace that a woman like me
is childless

oh don't you worry beautiful
i will father your children
the black nation must increase in number
fertility rates must go up
as chanted by the scarlet ibis

this raucous scarlet ibis
is the reason behind all this mess in our community
and surrounding townships
grab land it chanted before
and the people did
no thought to repercussions

oh i'd be damned
to let its long beak
determine what happens to my body
like what happened to my community
i'd be damned

scarlet ibis

Lover
Don't despair
Learn from Audre Lorde
Deliberate
Afraid of nothing
Change the narrative
Lauretta Ngcobo did
And they didn't die
Be the first if you must
Tell your stories
They might change lives
They might be rejected
Banning her work
Never stopped Miriam Tlali from writing
Stand up for yourself
Firmly
Darling it transcends

Be grateful
You are magnificent
Tell your stories

so
i learnt the mysteries of the tides
the wisdom of the moon
now
i am blooming

darling i am blooming
tides moon blooming

Bio/ About the author

Chief Operations Officer; *Brain Waves Development (NPO)*
**Reading towards a Master's Degree: MASTER OF
JOURNALISM NQF Level 9** *(Climate Change. Media
Reportage, Online News, Content Analysis): Tshwane
University of Technology*

BMIA Financial Journalism: *Bloomberg Philanthropies,
Gordon Institute of Business Science(GIBS) and Rhodes
University School of Journalism*
BTECH Journalism *(Media reporting and NDP2030): Tshwane
University of Technology*
Evaluating Social Programs: *Abdul Latif Jameel Poverty
Action Lab (J-PAL)*
**How to Manage an Evaluation, Commissioning Evaluation,
Deepening Evaluation**: *CLEAR Anglophone Africa*
NATDIP Journalism: *Tshwane University of Technology*

My mouth is the home of a rebellious poet
The rioting ground of revolutionary activists
Throne of the renaissance child
My mouth is the fortress of mighty feminists
Nursing from the nipples of a goddess
Lactating civil rights
Whose queen mother birthed both the sun and moon
Uprooting racism
Sexism
I am that foreseen descendent
Whose womb homes a mighty

Magnificent progeny
My mouth knows of
Foremothers with warrior fists
Stabbing colonialism
And for rooting, I thank You
Pouring bee sweetness
My mouth the carriage to an opulent tomorrow

Descendant of glorious Ancestors
The great granddaughter of divine foremothers –
Maria Baloyi (Ngwa Msisinyane), Elsie Ndhaba,
Moitsehi Rasego and Baleseng Chauke

I imagine they said
Little black girl welcome to the world
Where insecurities are wide mouthed and ready to
devour you
Systematic patriarchy isms and schisms in his
image ready to dismantle you
Darling
Kick ass

I hear them say

Grown black woman you walked the thorny miles
of life
Bleeding from your sole to your soul
Systematic patriarchy isms and schisms in his
image ready to dismantle you
Blurring your vision
Fight

Mighty black queen you have been conquering
through the struggles
Fixing your crown eyes weeping
Warrior queen
Unbowed
Magnificent black goddess
Thrive

Shaped by the history of the African people

From Miriam Tlali and Alice Walker's literary works on
gender and race, to historic inspirations – Charlotte
Mannye Maxeke and Pixley ka Isaka Seme

From the timeless music of Miriam Makeba and Nina
Simone to artworks against apartheid by Malangatana
Ngwenya and Thami Mnyele

From the ideals of black consciousness by Frantz Fanon
and Steve Biko to the stories of ordinary black women and
black men
Especially, heroic stories of black women who shaped Pan
African history - Lauretta Ngcobo, Bell Hooks, to the
undying story of Winifred Madikizela and those unknown

From the heart-breaking photographs of the June 16 1976
uprising and the March 21 1960 Sharpville massacre, to the
brutal killings of Mita Ngobeni and Emma Sathekge by
apartheid police in Atteridgeville
                    and
i, mikateko e. mbambo am a reminder that the cactus
blooms too

*Poems published first in, Africanization and Americanization Anthology. Volume 1: Searching for Inter-racial Interstitial, Inter-sectional, and Interstates meeting spaces (2018). Poetry contribution is under Part 8: Language, Identity, Colour and Colourism and Best "New" African Poets 2016 Anthology Poetry contribution is under Part 7: Tribute, Dedication and Women Rights

Publisher's list

If you have enjoyed *Blooming Cactus* consider these other fine books from Mwanaka Media and Publishing:

Cultural Hybridity and Fixity by Andrew Nyongesa
The Water Cycle by Andrew Nyongesa
Tintinnabulation of Literary Theory by Andrew Nyongesa
I Threw a Star in a Wine Glass by Fethi Sassi
South Africa and United Nations Peacekeeping Offensive Operations by Antonio Garcia
Africanization and Americanization Anthology Volume 1, Searching for Interracial, Interstitial, Intersectional and Interstates Meeting Spaces, Africa Vs North America by Tendai R Mwanaka
A Conversation…, A Contact by Tendai Rinos Mwanaka
A Dark Energy by Tendai Rinos Mwanaka
Africa, UK and Ireland: Writing Politics and Knowledge Production Vol 1 by Tendai R Mwanaka
Best New African Poets 2017 Anthology by Tendai R Mwanaka and Daniel Da Purificacao
Keys in the River: New and Collected Stories by Tendai Rinos Mwanaka
Logbook Written by a Drifter by Tendai Rinos Mwanaka
Mad Bob Republic: Bloodlines, Bile and a Crying Child by Tendai Rinos Mwanaka
How The Twins Grew Up/Makurire Akaita Mapatya by Milutin Djurickovic and Tendai Rinos Mwanaka
Writing Language, Culture and Development, Africa Vs Asia Vol 1 by Tendai R Mwanaka, Wanjohi wa Makokha and Upal Deb
Zimbolicious Poetry Vol 1 by Tendai R Mwanaka and Edward Dzonze

Zimbolicious: An Anthology of Zimbabwean Literature and Arts, Vol 3 by Tendai Mwanaka

Under The Steel Yoke by Jabulani Mzinyathi

A Case of Love and Hate by Chenjerai Mhondera

Epochs of Morning Light by Elena Botts

Fly in a Beehive by Thato Tshukudu

Bounding for Light by Richard Mbuthia

White Man Walking by John Eppel

A Cat and Mouse Affair by Bruno Shora

Sentiments by Jackson Matimba

Best New African Poets 2018 Anthology by Tendai R Mwanaka and Nsah Mala

Drawing Without Licence by Tendai R Mwanaka

Writing Grandmothers/ Escribiendo sobre nuestras raíces: Africa Vs Latin America Vol 2 by Tendai R Mwanaka and Felix Rodriguez

The Scholarship Girl by Abigail George

Words That Matter by Gerry Sikazwe

The Gods Sleep Through It All by Wonder Guchu

The Ungendered by Delia Watterson

The Big Noise and Other Noises by Christopher Kudyahakudadirwe

Tiny Human Protection Agency by Megan Landman

Ghetto Symphony by Mandla Mavolwane

Sky for a Foreign Bird by Fethi Sassi

A Portrait of Defiance by Tendai Rinos Mwanaka

When Escape Becomes the only Lover by Tendai R Mwanaka

Where I Belong: moments, mist and song by Smeetha Bhoumik

Nationalism: (Mis)Understanding Donald Trump's Capitalism, Racism, Global Politics, International Trade and Media Wars, Africa Vs North America Vol 2 by Tendai R Mwanaka

Of Bloom Smoke by Abigail George

Ashes by Ken Weene and Omar O Abdul

Ouafa and Thawra: About a Lover From Tunisia by Arturo Desimone

Thoughts Hunt The Loves/Pfungwa Dzinovhima Vadiwa by Jeton Kelmendi

وَالغَمَام...ويَسهَرُاللَّيلُعَلَىشَفَتِي by Fethi Sassi

A Letter to the President by Mbizo Chirasha

Righteous Indignation by Jabulani Mzinyathi:

This is Not a Poem by Richard Inya

Soon to be released

Notes From a Modern Chimurenga: Collected Stories by Tendai Rinos Mwanaka

Tom Boy by Megan Landman

My Spiritual Journey: A Study of the Emerald Tablets by Jonathan Thompson

Rhythm of Life by Olivia Ngozi Osouha

School of Love and Other Stories by Ricardo Felix Rodriguez

Cycle of Life by Ikegwu Michael Chukwudi

Denga reshiri yokunze kwenyika by Fethi Sassi

Because Sadness is Beautiful by Tanaka Chidora

PHENOMENOLOGY OF DECOLONIZING THE UNIVERSITY: Essays in the Contemporary Thoughts of Afrikology by Zvikomborero Kapuya

INFLUENCE OF CLIMATE VARIABILITY ON THE PREVALENCE OF DENGUE FEVER IN MANDERA COUNTY, KENYA by NDIWA JOSEPH KIMTAI

https://facebook.com/MwanakaMediaAndPublishing/

Printed in the United States
By Bookmasters